## Whatever Happened to Uncle Albert?

Anyone who likes to spot clues and solve problems will enjoy reading or acting in these four original plays.

Each play is different in tone: there is a Sherlock Holmes-style mystery, a werewolf transformation play, a contemporary slapstick mystery, and a play involving a trial. Beginning with the shortest and easiest to perform and ending with the longest and most complex, the author has taken into account the varying abilities and interests of the actors.

The plays require a minimum of props and furniture and can be staged in a classroom, a club meeting room, or at home. Young people will enjoy using their imaginations in developing the characters and deciding on costumes and makeup.

Tom Huffman's illustrations help to project the humor and suspense in the plays. And mystery buffs will be delighted to find a list of puzzling stories to read at the back of the book.

*Let the play begin.*

# WHATEVER HAPPENED TO UNCLE ALBERT?

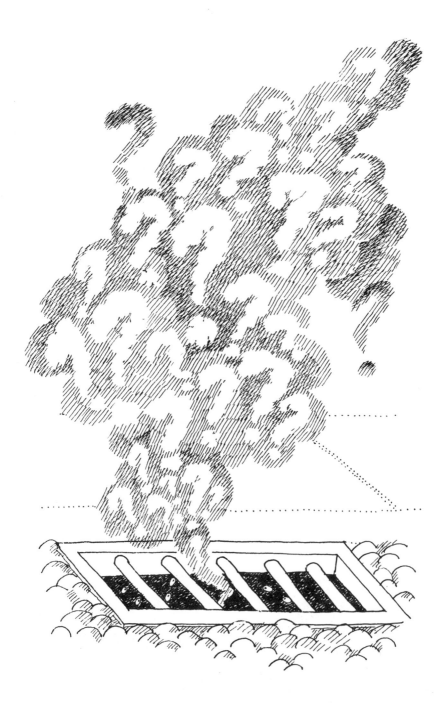

# WHATEVER HAPPENED TO UNCLE ALBERT?

## And Other Puzzling Plays

## by Sue Alexander
### Illustrations by Tom Huffman

 **Houghton Mifflin/Clarion Books/New York**

For Jim Giblin,
who is as much a part of this book as I am
—S.A.

To Sean and Shane
—T.H.

Houghton Mifflin/Clarion Books
52 Vanderbilt Avenue, New York, NY 10017

Text copyright© 1980 by Sue Alexander
Illustrations copyright© 1980 by Tom Huffman

**Library of Congress Cataloging in Publication Data**

Alexander, Sue, 1933–
Whatever happened to Uncle Albert?

1. Children's plays, American.
2. Detective and mystery plays, American.
I. Huffman, Tom. II. Title.
PS3551.L3576W47 812'.54 80-15075
ISBN 0-395-29104-6

# Contents

# A Note About This Book

The enjoyment of "play-acting" seems to be basic to human nature, whether we are participating on stage or in the audience. The opportunity to step out of oneself—to be someone else, even for a few minutes—is universally appealing. For young people, it's one area of endeavor that is greeted with complete enthusiasm whether as a school project or as a leisure-time activity.

The production of any play begins, but does not end, with the author's words. The creative imagination of the people involved—the players, the director, etc.—determines how successful the production will be. The four one-act plays in this book have been designed and written to allow for as much creative imagination as can be obtained within a dramatic structure. Simple sets, props, and stage directions make it possible to produce the plays in almost any location. Costuming has been left up to the players' resources and ingenuity.

Thematically, the plays reflect that part of all of us that likes to be scared or puzzled—temporarily. Each of the plays explores the theme with a different level of difficulty and with a different tone, taking into account the varying abilities and interests of the young people who will be involved. Underlying the whole book is a firm conviction that plays should be enjoyable to read, to produce, and to watch.

# To the Players

How good are you at spotting clues? At making deductions? At solving mysteries?

The one-act plays in this book will give you a chance to find out. And have fun while you're doing so.

You and some friends can put on these plays in your classroom at school, at a community center, or even in your backyard. The props that you will need are not hard to find. If you decide to perform the plays at school or a community center, most of the things you will need are already there. Only a few of them may have to be brought from home.

After you have read the plays, you and your friends can decide about costumes. You may feel that everyday clothes will do, or you may decide that certain characters should wear something special. You may decide that a character in one of the plays should have a charcoal mustache on his upper lip, or a character in another play should have powder on her hair to make her look older. These things are all up to you.

Part of the fun of putting on a play is the audience. Because these are mystery plays—and mysteries contain surprises—your audience will have more fun *if they don't know what the play is about before they watch it.* Do your rehearsing away from the people who will be your audience, and don't talk about the play before you're ready to present it. Then, when your audience is seated and waiting:

LET THE PLAY BEGIN!

# WHATEVER HAPPENED TO UNCLE ALBERT?

# THE GHOST OF PLYMOUTH CASTLE

## Characters

Narrator
Blaylock Jones, detective
Datson, Jones' friend
Lady Plymouth
Kevin, Lady Plymouth's cousin
Prunella, Kevin's fiancée
Police officer

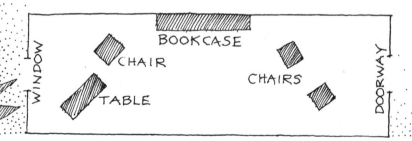

LADY PLYMOUTH     KEVIN     PRUNELLA     POLICE OFFICER

### Setting, properties, production notes

The scene is the parlor of Plymouth Castle. There are three chairs, a table, and a bookcase in the room. On the table are three squares of cloth. Jones carries a magnifying glass. Datson has a handkerchief in his pocket. The ghost wears an old sheet.

The doorway is to the audience's right, the window is to the audience's left. Characters enter and exit on the doorway side except where noted.

**As the play begins** _____

The narrator is standing on the window side at the front of the stage area. After he speaks, he exits on the window side.

**Narrator:** Everyone, I'm sure, has heard of that famous detective, Sherlock Holmes. Have you also heard of another detective, Blaylock Jones? No? Well, then you will hear about him now. Hmmm. I suppose the best way is for you to watch Blaylock Jones and his friend, Datson, solve the mystery of THE GHOST OF PLYMOUTH CASTLE.

*(Jones enters, followed by Datson. Jones wanders around the room, looking at everything through his magnifying glass. Datson sits down and looks around.)*

**Datson:** I say, Jones, what makes you think that Lady Plymouth believes this castle of hers is haunted?

**Jones:** Elementary, my dear Datson. When she visited us in my office, she jumped when the door-chain clanked.

**Datson:** (*He looks around the room.*) Well, I wouldn't be surprised if there *was* a ghost here. This castle is very spooky.

(*Lady Plymouth enters. Datson stands up.*)

**Lady Plymouth:** Mr. Jones! And Datson! It's so good of you to come. Do sit down.

(*Jones and Datson bow toward Lady Plymouth and then sit down.*)

**Jones:** Lady Plymouth, you said you had a problem. What is it?

**Lady Plymouth:** (*She walks back and forth, nervously wringing her hands while she is talking.*) My uncle's will stated that I was to inherit this castle—but only if I stayed here alone for forty-four nights. I've been here now for forty of those nights—but I'm not sure I can stay even *one* more!

**Jones:** Because of a ghost?

**Lady Plymouth:** (*She gasps.*) How did you know? (*She sits down on a chair and stares at Jones.*)

**Jones:** (*He stands up and bows.*) I am Blaylock Jones, Madam.

**Lady Plymouth:** Oh, of course! I should have known. Somehow you find out *everything*, don't you?

**Datson:** Yes. That's elementary.

**Jones:** Now, tell us about the ghost, Lady Plymouth.

**Lady Plymouth:** It began last week. I heard chains clanking in the night. At first I thought I was dreaming. But you can't have the same dream every night, can you?

**Datson:** It isn't likely. But it might be possible.

(*While Datson is talking, Jones is looking at Lady Plymouth through his magnifying glass.*)

**Jones:** Perhaps, Datson. But I deduce there was more than just the sound of clanking chains. Am I right, Lady Plymouth?

**Lady Plymouth:** You're marvelous, Mr. Jones! How did you know?

**Jones:** Blaylock Jones knows a great many things. Besides, the fright is still in your eyes.

**Datson:** Oh, I thought you had spotted a bug, Jones. There seems to be one in MY eye. (*He rubs his eye.*)

**Jones:** (*He goes close to Datson and looks through the magnifying glass at Datson's eye.*) So there is. It appears to be a gnat. Use your handkerchief in the right corner, Datson, and you'll have it.

**Datson:** (*He takes out his handkerchief and dabs at the corner of his eye.*) Got it! Thank you, Jones. (*He puts his handkerchief away.*)

**Jones:** (*He turns toward Lady Plymouth.*) Now, Lady Plymouth. What happened next?

**Lady Plymouth:** (*She stands and walks over to the table and picks up the cloth squares.*) I began to find these.

**Jones:** (*He takes the squares and looks at them through his magnifying glass.*) Hmmm. The same message on all of them. GO AWAY! And they are signed THE GHOST OF PLYMOUTH CASTLE.

**Datson:** My word! Let me see them, Jones. (*He gets up and takes the squares from Jones. He holds them up close to his face.*) My word! Oh! Ah— ah—ACHOO! Achoo! (*He drops the squares.*) Oh, dear! Achoo! (*He pulls his handkerchief out and holds it to his nose.*) ACHOO!

(*Jones bends over and picks up the squares and puts them on the table.*)

**Datson:** (*He blows his nose and then puts his handkerchief away.*) Pardon me. I AM sorry. I don't know what brought that on.

**Jones:** No matter, Datson. We have more important things to think about. (*He turns toward Lady Plymouth.*) Then what happened?

**Lady Plymouth:** The most terrible thing of all! (*She puts her hands over her face and then takes them down.*) I SAW THE GHOST! I heard a noise and came downstairs—and I SAW IT!

**Jones:** Where?

**Lady Plymouth:** In this room.

**Datson:** My word! (*He jumps up and looks under his chair.*) Nothing there. That's a relief!

**Jones:** Lady Plymouth's ghost appeared in the *night,* Datson.

**Datson:** Oh! I didn't think of that. (*He sits down.*)

(*Offstage: someone knocks loudly on a door.*)

**Lady Plymouth:** Oh! That must be my cousin Kevin and his fiancée! They've taken to dropping in almost every day at this time. Mr. Jones, I haven't told Kevin about the ghost. I don't want to worry him. With his wedding coming up, he has enough on his mind.

**Jones:** Don't worry, Lady Plymouth. Neither Datson nor I will mention the ghost.

(*Lady Plymouth goes out. Then she comes back, followed by Kevin and Prunella.*)

**Lady Plymouth:** Kevin, Prunella, I'd like you to meet Blaylock Jones and his friend, Datson.

**Jones:** (*He stands up and shakes Kevin's hand.*) How do you do?

**Datson:** (*He gets up and goes over to Prunella to shake her hand, but before he can do so, he starts to sneeze.*) Ah . . . ah . . . ahchoo! Oh dear! (*He takes out his handkerchief.*) Pardon me! Achoo! (*He blows his nose.*)

**Jones:** (*He goes over to Prunella and shakes her hand. Then he sniffs the air.*) Lovely perfume you're wearing. Essence of violets, isn't it?

**Prunella:** Why, yes!

**Datson:** Violets! No wonder I sneezed! I'm allergic to violets! (*He blows his nose again. Then he backs away from Prunella.*)

**Kevin:** (*He sits down.*) I say, Cousin, is something wrong? Is that why a famous detective like Blaylock Jones is visiting you?

**Lady Plymouth:** Well . . .

**Prunella:** Maybe it's something to do with the will. Are you, perhaps, thinking of leaving here, Lady Plymouth? If you do, then Kevin will inherit the castle, won't he?

**Lady Plymouth:** (*She speaks sadly.*) Yes, Prunella. And I would have no home at all.

**Prunella:** That would be too bad. (*She goes over to the window side of the room.*) Would you mind if I opened the window? It's a bit stuffy in here.

**Lady Plymouth:** Go right ahead, Prunella. Would anyone like some tea?

(*Prunella pantomimes opening a window.*)

**Kevin:** We really can't stay. We're on our way to a party. I just wanted to drop in for a moment. (*He stands up.*) Come on, Prunella.

**Jones:** Datson and I must go too, Lady Plymouth.

**Lady Plymouth:** But . . . !

**Jones:** Don't worry, Lady Plymouth. I'll take care of that matter we were discussing.

**Lady Plymouth:** Oh! All right, Mr. Jones. I'll see you to the door.

(*Everyone goes off, saying good-bye to each other.*)

**Narrator:** (*He enters and stands on the doorway side.*) A bit later that evening, Blaylock Jones and Datson returned to Plymouth Castle. But they didn't knock on the door. Instead, they climbed in the window that Prunella had opened. (*He goes off the doorway side.*)

(*Jones comes in first, followed by Datson.*)

**Jones:** (*He speaks in a loud whisper.*) All right, Datson. You get behind that chair and I'll get behind this one.

(*Datson scrunches down behind the chair near the window. Jones scrunches down behind the chair nearest the doorway.*)

**Datson:** Er . . . I say, Jones, is there such a thing as a REAL ghost?

**Jones:** We shall see, Datson, we shall see. Be quiet now.

**Ghost:** (*It enters from window side and moves slowly toward doorway.*) Ooooh! Oooooooh! OOOOOOOOOH!

**Jones:** (*He stands up.*) Grab it, Datson!

**Datson:** (*He jumps up and grabs at the ghost—and misses. He begins to sneeze.*) ACHOO! Achoo!

(*The ghost tries to run out the doorway, but is grabbed by Jones.*)

**Jones:** I've got you!

**Lady Plymouth:** (*She runs in.*) What . . . ! The ghost! Mr. Jones! Datson! Oh, dear! Mr. Jones, I thought you'd *gone.*

**Jones:** So did your ghost. Allow me to introduce you, Lady Plymouth. (*He pulls the sheet off the ghost.*)

**Lady Plymouth:** Prunella!

**Jones:** Exactly so.

**Datson:** My word!

**Jones:** Yes. Prunella was determined to live in this castle.

**Prunella:** (*She speaks angrily.*) I would have too, if it weren't for you, Mr. Jones!

**Lady Plymouth:** Oh, dear!

**Jones:** Lady Plymouth, I alerted the police when I realized that Prunella was the ghost. They should be outside now. Would you let them in, please?

**Lady Plymouth:** Of course. (*She goes out, and returns followed by a police officer who takes Prunella out.*)

**Datson:** I don't see, Jones, how you knew it was Prunella.

**Jones:** Elementary, my dear Datson. You sneezed.

**Datson:** What?

**Jones:** Yes, Datson. Your allergy to violets caused you to sneeze when Prunella, or anything she handled, was near you.

**Lady Plymouth:** You mean the cloth messages! Datson *did* sneeze while he was looking at them!

**Jones:** Exactly, Lady Plymouth. And I was sure of it after Prunella left the window open so that, as the ghost, she could get in.

**Datson:** My word! I solved the mystery—and I didn't even know it!

**Jones:** You might say it was elementary, Datson.

*(All three go out.)*

**Narrator:** *(He comes to center stage.)* And so ended the mystery of the Ghost of Plymouth Castle.

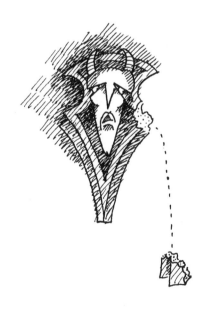

# WHATEVER HAPPENED TO UNCLE ALBERT?

## Characters

Mary Green
George Green, Mary's brother
Clark, the handyman
Henry Brink
Agnes Brink, Henry's wife

## Setting, properties, production notes

The scene is the living room of Uncle Albert's house. There are three chairs, a small table, a desk-size table, and a bookcase filled with books. One of the books is a dictionary. There are papers and magazines on the tables.

The window is to the audience's left; the doorway is to the audience's right. Characters enter and exit on the doorway side of the stage area.

5

**As the play begins** _____

Mary enters, followed by George.

_____

**Mary:** George, I don't think it was fair of Mother to insist that we come out here! Just because she couldn't get Uncle Albert on the phone! It's already four o'clock, and I have a date tonight!

**George:** You're the one who's being unfair, Mary. After all, Mother is in the hospital. She couldn't come herself, could she? And it isn't just that she couldn't get Uncle Albert on the phone. *Nobody* has heard from him! Even his lawyer was worried enough to call us and ask if we knew where he was. Besides, we aren't that far from the city. It only took us an hour to get here.

**Mary:** I don't care how long it took. I don't like coming here. It's too quiet. There's never anything interesting to do, unless it's to count all the different kinds of bugs that live in the bushes. And it smells funny up here, too.

**George:** That funny smell, my dear sister, is fresh air. If you had spent more of your eighteen years out of the city, you'd recognize it.

**Clark:** (*He enters and stands in doorway.*) You the folks the lawyer fella called me about? Mr. Manero's niece and nephew? The lawyer fella said I was to come down and see that you got in all right.

**Mary:** (*She turns toward Clark.*) Oh! You must be Clark, the handyman. Mother told me about you.

**George:** Maybe you can help us, Clark. We're supposed to find out where Uncle Albert is. Do you know?

**Clark:** (*He comes a couple of steps farther into the room.*) Nope. Told that lawyer that I didn't. Haven't seen him in quite a while. Don't never come here unless Mr. Manero calls. Too many strange going's on for me.

**George:** What do you mean, Clark? Sit down and tell us.

**Clark:** (*He sits down on the chair nearest to the doorway and looks around uneasily.*) Mostly, it's the animal noises that I don't like.

**Mary:** (*She sits down.*) Animal noises? I didn't know Uncle Albert had any pets.

**Clark:** That's just it. He don't. At least, none that ever come out in the day. But I hear them at night, oftentimes. Ain't natural—animals you can hear but never see.

**George:** What makes you think the noises come from *here?*

**Clark:** There's no other place for them to come from that I'd hear them. Closest other house is the Brinks', and that's a mile or more down the road.

**George:** Hmmm. That *is* strange. (*He walks back and forth, thinking. Then he stops and looks at Clark.*) Clark, when did you see Uncle Albert last?

**Clark:** (*He scratches his head and thinks.*) Well, best as I can recall, it was the same day as the ruckus with the wolf.

**Mary:** (*She jumps up.*) Wolf! What wolf! Around *here?*

**George:** Mary, calm down. Go on, Clark. You were saying, "It was the same day . . ."

**Clark:** Yep. Night police patrol found a wolf stalking the Brinks' hen house and shot it. Funny thing, that. Never been a wolf in these parts before. Can't nobody figure out where it came from. Big one, too. Took three shotgun blasts to kill it.

**Mary:** (*She sits down in the chair, shivers, and hugs herself.*) George, I don't like this. I want to go home!

**George:** Not yet, Mary. This is getting interesting. When was this, Clark? Two weeks ago? Longer than that? When?

**Clark:** (*He scratches his head, counts on his fingers, and mumbles to himself.*) Now I remember. It was a month ago—exactly. Was a full moon then too—just like there's to be tonight. That's how I know. Follow the moon's coming and going in the paper every day.

**George:** And you haven't seen or heard from Uncle Albert since?

**Clark:** Nope. Nary a word. Don't surprise me none, though. He's a strange one, all right. Always poking through those musty old books of his. Don't have time for friendly conversation a-tall. Just, "Clark, the door needs painting." Then back to his books. Never did see so many scratches on a door. Like some wild animal been at it. Took two coats of paint to cover up them scratches. (*He stands up.*) Well, if you've no more need of me, I'll be going. Got my own chores to do. (*He starts toward the doorway.*)

**George:** Thank you, Clark. We'll lock up when we leave.

(*Clark exits. Mary and George watch him go.*)

**Mary:** George, he scares me.

**George:** Don't be silly, Mary. He just likes to talk, that's all. It *is* kind of lonely up here. And Uncle Albert isn't the world's greatest conversation-maker, as I remember.

(*He wanders over to the bookcase and runs his finger along the spines of a few books.*)

Funny thing about these old books, though. The few times we've been here, it seemed as if Uncle Albert deliberately kept me from looking at them. I wonder why?

**Mary:** Probably because once you get your nose in a book you never come up for air until it's time to leave. Speaking of leaving, why don't we? We can tell Mother that we came and looked and Uncle Albert isn't here, that's all.

**George:** (*He shakes his head to indicate no.*) We haven't really looked to see *why* he isn't here. Tell you what, Mary. You go upstairs and see if you can find travel brochures or anything like that. I'll look around down here. Uncle Albert didn't just disappear into thin air!

**Mary:** Oh, all right! But then, let's go. It's after five, now. My date is at eight o'clock and I still have a million things to do. (*She goes out.*)

**George:** (*He goes over to the table and shuffles through the papers and magazines.*) Hmmm. Nothing here. Just some old wildlife magazines. And a butcher's bill. (*He picks it up.*) Uncle Albert sure eats a lot of meat!

*(He puts the bill down and wanders over to the bookcase. He takes out a book, flips through it, puts it back and then takes out another.)*

What a strange title for a book—*Incantations for the Full Moon*. What does incantation mean? There must be a dictionary here somewhere.

*(He puts the book down on top of the bookcase and takes out the dictionary.)*

Here it is. *(He flips through the dictionary.)* Now, let's see. In . . . incan . . . found it. Incantation: magic spell.

*(He puts the dictionary away and picks up the book from the top of the bookcase.)*

Magic spells? *Uncle Albert?* Hmmm . . .

*(He goes over to the chair and sits down and begins to read.)*

**Mary:** *(She enters.)* George, I didn't find anything *like* a travel brochure. *(She stops.)* George!

**George:** *(He doesn't look up.)* I hear you, Mary. Sit down. I want to read you something.

**Mary:** You want to *what?* Big brother, you're too much! I'm going to be late for my date and you want to *read* me something!

**George:** It will only take a minute. Come on, sit down.

**Mary:** I might as well. I can see you're going to read it to me whether I want you to or not. (*She sits down.*)

**George:** This is a book—believe it or not—of magic spells. Listen to this one. It's for turning oneself into a wolf.

**Mary:** A wolf! I don't want to hear it!

**George:** Come on, Mary, it's only a book. Just listen. It goes like this:

> Tails and paws, fangs and claws
> Yellowed eyes and giant maws
> Three times 'round 'neath the moon
> Lupine fur will follow soon.

**Mary:** (*She jumps up.*) That's horrible! It gives me the shivers! Put that book away and let's get out of here!

**George:** In a minute. I want to read a little bit more.

**Mary:** Oh, George, you're impossible! I'm going to get a drink of water and then we're going! (*She goes out.*)

**George:** (*He closes the book, puts it on the table and gets up. He walks back and forth a few times across the room.*) Let's see now, how did that go? (*He stops and thinks.*) I've got it:

> Tails and paws, fangs and claws
> Yellowed eyes and giant maws
> Three times 'round 'neath the moon
> Lupine fur will follow soon.

(*He walks over to the window side and looks out.*) Hmmm. The moon will be up full in a minute or two. I wonder . . . (*He turns and goes out quickly.*)

(*The stage area remains empty for a minute.*)

**Henry:** (*He stands at the doorway looking into the room. Agnes is at his side.*) Hello! Hello! Anyone home? Mr. Manero? Albert?

**Agnes:** I *told* you I saw lights, Henry. And the door is wide open. He *must* be back. (*She comes further into the room. Henry follows her.*)

**Mary:** (*She enters.*) George, who are you talking . . . oh!

**Henry:** I beg your pardon. We don't mean to intrude. I'm Henry Brink. And this is my wife, Agnes. We're neighbors of Mr. Manero's. Is he in?

**Mary:** The Brinks . . . oh, yes! Clark mentioned you. You live down the road. No, my Uncle Albert isn't here. I'm Mary Green, his niece.

**Agnes:** How do you do. I do hope you'll forgive us, walking in like this. But the door was open . . .

**Mary:** Where's George?

**Agnes:** George?

**Mary:** My brother. He was in here a minute ago. (*She looks around.*)

**Henry:** (*He sits down. So does Agnes.*) Have you heard from your uncle? Is that why you're here?

**Mary:** No, we've not heard a word. Nobody has. Clark says he's been gone a whole month!

**Henry:** (*He nods his head.*) That's right, it *is* about a month. We last saw him the day before the wolf tried to get at our hens. Albert had come over to take a look at the new incubator we'd installed in the hen house. Very interested, he is, in the experimental chicken-breeding we've been doing. Drops in quite often to see how it's going.

**Agnes:** When we didn't hear from him after a while, I thought he might be ill. So I came over to see. When I got here, the door was standing open and the house was empty. I called the police, but they thought I was just imagining that anything was wrong. They said he probably went on a trip somewhere and just forgot to close the door.

**Mary:** That's what George thinks, too. (*She looks around again.*) I wonder where my brother is? Would you excuse me a minute? I'll see if I can find him.

**Agnes:** She seems like a nice girl. Not at all strange—like her uncle. (*She gets up and walks over to the table and shuffles through the magazines and papers on the table.*)

**Henry:** Agnes, you're not being kind.

**Agnes:** Truthful, though. I never saw a man with such strange eyes. Almost like an animal's. Slitted—and with a yellow cast to them.

**Mary:** (*She enters.*) I can't find George anywhere! And I've looked in every room of the house!

**Henry:** I wouldn't worry if I were you. He probably just stepped into the garden. . . .

*(Offstage: the sound of howling.)*

**Mary:** (*She screams and jumps up.*) What was that?

**Henry:** (*He runs to the window.*) Sounds like some kind of wild animal! (*He looks out of the window.*) I don't see anything, though. . . .

**Agnes:** Henry, you don't suppose it's another . . .

**Henry:** Wolf? Not likely. How that one got anywhere around here is still a puzzle. Still, it does *sound* like a wolf, doesn't it?

**Mary:** Oh, where is George! (*She sinks into the chair and starts to cry.*)

**Henry:** Don't worry, young lady. I'm sure he'll be right back.

*(George stands just inside doorway, looking in.)*

**Mary:** (*She looks up and sees George. She jumps up.*) George! Where were you? I looked all over for you!

*(George doesn't answer. He moves slowly, stealthily toward a chair.)*

**Mary:** George! What's wrong with you? Are you sick? (*She gets up and goes over to him. She reaches out her hand toward his arm. George pushes her hand away and sits down.*)

**George:** (*He speaks slowly, haltingly, as if speaking is difficult.*) Leave—me—alone. I'm—all—right.

**Mary:** You don't sound all right! Where were you? George, you look awful!

**George:** (*He is shouting.*) I'm—all—right, I—tell you! Leave me alone!

**Agnes:** (*She gets up and takes Henry's arm.*) Henry, let's go.

**Henry:** Yes, my dear. (*They start to walk out.*)

**Agnes:** (*She speaks in a loud whisper.*) Did you notice his eyes? That yellow cast to them? (*They go out.*)

**Mary:** (*She sits down facing George.*) George, what's wrong with you? You're scaring me!

**George:** I've—I've—had an unusual experience, Mary. Give me a minute. I'll be all right. (*He puts his head in his hands.*)

**Mary:** (*She gets up and walks back and forth.*) George, please, let's go. I don't even care about missing my date. I'm just scared. First, Uncle Albert disappears, then this strange neighborhood with wolves getting shot and strange animals howling—and now you, acting like this. . . .

**George:** (*He puts his hands down. He sounds like himself again.*) It's all right, Mary. There's an explanation for all of it.

**Mary:** (*She stops and looks at George.*) Are you going to tell me what it is?

**George:** (*He gets up and goes over to Mary. He takes her hand.*) I think it will be better if I *show* you, Mary. Come, stand over here, where the moonlight is coming in the window. (*He leads her to a spot in front of the window.*) Now, I want you to say what I say and do what I do.

**Mary:** George, what . . . ?

**George:** Please, Mary. No questions. I promise that you'll understand everything.

**Mary:** Oh, all right!

**George:** Good. (*He turns Mary until they are facing each other.*) Now, listen carefully and remember to do exactly what I do. Let's begin.

Tails and paws, fangs and claws . . .

**Mary:** Tails and paws, fangs and claws . . .

**George:** Yellowed eyes and giant maws . . .

**Mary:** Yellowed eyes and giant maws . . .

**George:** Three times 'round 'neath the moon . . . (*He turns three times.*)

**Mary:** Three times 'round 'neath the moon . . . (*She turns three times.*)

**George:** Lupine fur will follow soon. (*Slowly he begins to hunch over.*)

**Mary:** Lupine fur will follow soon. (*She begins to hunch over.*) George! What's happening? I feel so strange! (*She hunches more, gets closer to the floor.*) George! My hands! They're turning into claws! And I'm growing fur! (*She looks at George who is on his hands and knees.*) George! You've turned into a . . . Oh, no! Now, I know what happened to Uncle Albert . . . (*Her voice trails off into a wolf's howl. George joins with a howl too, and they go off on hands and knees, howling.*)

# THE MYSTERY OF THE STONE STATUES

## Characters

Narrator
Sidney Stalwart
Dr. Amos Chilling
Amy Truegood
The President of Wakowako

## Setting, properties, production notes

The scene is Dr. Chilling's laboratory. There is·a table, a stool, and two chairs. Beakers, glasses, three or four bottles, mixers, spoons, a pencil and papers are on the table. Each bottle has some water, colored with food coloring, in it. A key is taped to the underside of the table. Sidney carries a folder of papers and has a calling card in his pocket. Offstage there is a plate of cookies.

The closet is to the audience's left, and doorway is to the audience's right. Characters enter and exit on the doorway side except where noted.

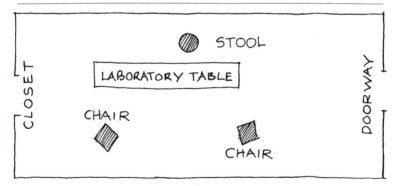

**As the play begins**_____

The narrator is standing in the front of the stage area, toward the closet side. Sidney is standing on the doorway side. Dr. Chilling is sitting on the stool at the table. Dr. Chilling and Sidney are motionless as the Narrator speaks. Dr. Chilling remains motionless during Sidney's first speech.

**Narrator:** While on vacation, Sidney Stalwart, Topnotch Secret Detective for the Worldwide Secret Detective Agency, received a telegram. It said:

> *To:* Sidney Stalwart, Topnotch Secret Detective
> *From:* Boss of Worldwide Secret Detective Agency
> Sidney,
> We've had a report that Evil Scientist, Dr. Amos Chilling, intends to do away with the President of Wakowako and take over that country. Secret Detective Amy Truegood was sent to Dr. Chilling's laboratory to investigate and hasn't been heard from since. Your job: Stop Chilling. Also, find Amy. P.S. Also see if

you can find out what happened to the dog catcher. He was last seen knocking on Dr. Chilling's door.

*(The Narrator goes off on the closet side.)*

**Sidney:** In my disguise as a magazine reporter, Dr. Chilling will never guess that I'm really Sidney Stalwart, Topnotch Secret Detective! *(He goes off on the doorway side.)*

**Chilling:** *(He pours liquid from bottle to beaker, then adds a drop from another bottle, stirs the mixture, adds another drop from a different bottle and stirs again.)* Nothing will stop me now! I've tested my formula on forty-two nosy people and it worked every time! Soon I'll test this new supply on that snoopy Secret Detective locked in my closet—and then it will be ready to use to put the country of Wakowako in my power!

*(Offstage: a rapping on a door.)*

**Chilling:** Hmmm. Can that be the President of Wakowako? He's an hour early! Well, no matter. I'm ready for him. *(He raises his voice.)* Come in, the door is open!

**Sidney:** *(He enters.)* Dr. Chilling, I presume?

**Chilling:** Who are *you?*

**Sidney:** (*He comes further into the room and pulls the calling card out of his pocket.*) My card. (*He hands it to Chilling.*)

**Chilling:** (*He reads the card.*) Sidney Stalwart, *Fame Magazine*. Magazine! I don't want any subscriptions!

**Sidney:** Well, that's not *exactly* why I'm here. *Fame Magazine* was told that you're a Very Important Person.

**Chilling:** That's true. Very true. I AM very important. And after today I might just become the most important person in the world. (*He rubs his hands together gleefully.*)

**Sidney:** Is that so? In that case, I'm sure you won't mind answering some questions. After all, an interview in *Fame Magazine* will make you famous as well as important.

**Chilling:** Hmmm. I've always wanted to be famous. *Fame Magazine,* you say? Come in, come in, Mr. Stalwart! Sit down! You understand that I'm a busy man. And I'm expecting a guest to arrive soon. But I can't deny the world the pleasure of knowing about me—so I'll answer your questions.

**Sidney:** I had a feeling you would. (*He sits down on a chair, opens his folder, and shuffles the papers. One paper drops to the floor, but he doesn't notice it.*) Let's see, that list of questions is here somewhere. (*He shuffles the papers some more and then pulls out a single sheet of paper.*) All right, first question. Are you ready?

**Chilling:** Yes, yes. Get on with it. (*He coughs.*)

**Sidney:** (*He reads from the paper.*) Will you go to the movies with me on Saturday?

**Chilling:** WILL I WHAT? (*He coughs again.*)

**Sidney:** I said, will you ... Oh! Sorry, wrong paper. (*He looks carefully at it.*) Hmmm. Amy never did answer me. Now I know why. I forgot to give her the question. Hmmm.

**Chilling:** Mr. Stalwart! Will you please get on with the interview! I'm a very busy man, you know. (*He coughs several times.*)

**Sidney:** That's a bad cough you have. Did you ever try molasses and honey? It's good for your throat.

**Chilling:** (*He coughs once more.*) Never mind my throat. Just ask your questions.

**Sidney:** (*He shuffles the papers in the folder again.*) That list of questions is here somewhere. (*He pulls out another sheet of paper.*) Here it is. First question: Do you live by yourself?

**Chilling:** Yes. I'm all alone here.

**Sidney:** (*He looks in his pockets and in the folder.*) Hmmm. What did I do with that pencil? (*He looks up.*) You wouldn't happen to have an extra pencil, would you?

**Chilling:** For a reporter, you're not very well prepared. (*He takes the pencil from his table and gives it to Sidney.*)

**Sidney:** Thank you. Now where were we? Uh . . . you were saying that you were alone here.

**Chilling:** That's right.

**Sidney:** Actually, that's wrong. I'm here.

**Chilling:** But you're interviewing me!

**Sidney:** I know that. But I'm *here*. Now, did you leave out anyone else?

**Chilling:** (*He shakes his head in confusion.*) No. (*He coughs.*)

**Sidney:** You really ought to do something about that cough. How about molasses and lemon?

**Chilling:** Mr. Stalwart! Please! Just ask your questions!

**Sidney:** If you insist. (*He looks at the paper again.*) Next question. How many rooms are there in your house?

**Chilling:** Forty-two.

**Sidney:** Are you sure about that?

**Chilling:** Of course! I live here, don't I?

**Sidney:** Yes. But since you didn't know how many people were here, you may be wrong about the number of rooms, too. And you want the readers of *Fame Magazine* to have the right answers, don't you?

**Chilling:** With you asking the questions, I don't think that's possible. (*He sighs and shakes his head.*) Do you want to count the rooms yourself?

**Sidney:** Now that's an idea!

**Chilling:** (*He sighs again.*) Very well, go ahead.

(*Sidney gets up and goes out.*)

**Chilling:** (*He comes out from behind the table and walks back and forth.*) There's something strange about that reporter. (*He looks down and sees the piece of paper that Sidney dropped.*) What's this? (*He bends down and picks it up.*) It's a telegram. (*He reads it to himself.*) Reporter, indeed! Another one of those snoopy Secret Detectives! Well, this new supply of my formula will take care of both of them! (*He goes back behind the table and mixes the water some more and then pours it into a glass.*)

**Sidney:** (*He enters.*) You were right. There *are* forty-two rooms. This is a very interesting house. Did you know that there are stone statues in every room?

**Chilling:** Yes, of course, I know! I—ah—*collect* them.

**Sidney:** All the statues have drinking glasses in their hands. And one of them has a dog-catcher's cap on. It's a special kind of collection, isn't it?

**Chilling:** Yes. A VERY special collection.

**Sidney:** The readers of *Fame Magazine* will want to know that. (*He opens his folder and pulls out a sheet of paper and pencil. Then he sits down and begins to write.*) Dr. Chilling collects stone statues.

**Chilling:** You look a bit warm, Mr. Stalwart. Would you like a glass of iced tea? (*He holds out the glass he has filled.*)

**Sidney:** That's very nice of you. It *is* a bit warm in here. (*He takes the glass, but does not drink.*)

**Chilling:** That should cool you off—for a long time.

**Sidney:** Er—I hate to be a bother, Dr. Chilling. But you wouldn't happen to have any cookies, would you? Iced tea tastes better when I have something sweet with it—like cookies.

**Chilling:** Cookies! (*He sighs.*) Very well. I think there are some in the kitchen. I'll get them. (*He goes out, shaking his head.*)

**Sidney:** There must be a place where Dr. Chilling keeps all of his secrets. All I have to do is find it. (*He gets up and goes over to the laboratory table. He puts the glass down and begins to pick up the other things on the table and look at them and then put them down. He glances around the room.*)

**President:** (*He sits down.*) Do not hurry yourself, Dr. Chilling. My journey has been a long one. I should welcome a few moments of rest.

**Sidney:** Er . . . would you like a cookie, Mr. President? They look very good. (*He offers the plate to the President.*)

**President:** Thank you. (*He takes a cookie.*) But really, I am thirsty. You will not mind if I drink this? (*He picks up the glass and begins to lift it to his mouth.*)

**Sidney:** Mr. President!

**President:** (*He lowers the glass and looks at Sidney.*) Yes?

**Sidney:** Ah—Mr. President, you don't want to drink that.

**President:** I beg your pardon?

**Sidney:** There's a fly in it.

**President:** A fly? (*He looks into the glass.*) I don't see any fly.

**Sidney:** No? Well, it's one of those very small ones. You know, the kind that bite when you're not looking. I wouldn't want you to get a bite on your tongue. I had one once, right here. . . . (*He sticks out his tongue at the President and points to a spot on it.*)

**Chilling:** (*He coughs.*) Mr. President! I think that before you drink anything we ought to sign the papers.

**President:** Perhaps you are right, Dr. Chilling. (*He puts the glass down on the table.*) After all, that is why I am here.

**Chilling:** (*He shuffles through the papers some more.*) I was *sure* those papers were here! (*He coughs again.*)

**Sidney:** Your cough is getting worse, Dr. Chilling. If I were you . . .

**Chilling:** (*He coughs several times.*) That's one thing I can be thankful for, Stalwart. You are NOT me! Excuse me, Mr. President. I must have taken the papers into the other room. I'll go get them. (*He goes out, coughing.*)

Hmmm. I didn't see that closet before. Maybe his secrets are in there. (*He goes to the closet side and pantomimes trying to open the door.*) It's locked! Hmmm. If I were the key to the closet, where would I be? Of course! Under the table! (*He reaches under the table and gets the key.*) I'm not called Sidney Stalwart, Topnotch Secret Detective for nothing! (*He goes to the closet side and pantomimes opening the door. He backs up as Amy Truegood comes out of the closet.*)

**Amy:** Oh, Sidney! Thank goodness! I thought I'd never get out of there!

**Sidney:** I'm surprised at you, Amy Truegood. Hiding in that closet. You know this is no time to be playing hide and seek. Especially since the Boss is worried about you.

**Amy:** Sidney, I wasn't—oh, dear. Sidney, there's no time to lose. The President of Wakowako will be here soon. We have to stop Dr. Chilling!

**Sidney:** I think you and the Boss are imagining things, Amy. Dr. Chilling seems to be a very nice man. He even noticed that I was warm and fixed me a glass of iced tea. And now he's gone to get me some cookies to have with it.

**Amy:** Sidney, Dr. Chilling is *not* nice! He's invented something that turns people into STONE STATUES!

**Sidney:** So *that's* where he got his collection.

**Amy:** And that's how he's planning to take over the country of Wakowako. Dr. Chilling is going to get the President to sign some papers giving him the right to rule the country. Then the President will be turned into stone too!

**Sidney:** And Dr. Chilling will have another statue for his collection. Hmmm. I wonder what room he'll put it in?

**Amy:** Sidney!

**Sidney:** You're right, Amy. We're going to have to stop Dr. Chilling. (*He walks back and forth, picks up the glass as if to drink, then he thinks of something that he wants to say, and he lowers the glass.*) You know, all those stone statues have drinking glasses in their hands. What Dr. Chilling has invented must be in something you drink.

**Amy:** Like that iced tea.

**Sidney:** Yes, Like this iced . . . (*He looks at the glass in his hand and then quickly puts it down.*) I don't think I'm thirsty anymore.

**Amy:** Sidney, those papers must be in this room. Dr. Chilling had them in his hand when he shoved me in that closet. (*She goes over to the table and looks for them.*) Here they are! (*She picks them up and brings them over to Sidney.*)

**Sidney:** (*He reads the papers to himself and then looks up.*) Very clever. What the President of Wakowako *thinks* he's signing is an agreement with Dr. Chilling to start a zoo in his country. But in the fine print . . .

**Amy:** Sidney! I hear footsteps! Dr. Chilling must be coming back!

**Sidney:** I'll think of something, Amy. In the meantime you get back in the closet! And take these with you! (*He shoves the papers into her hand.*) Hurry!

(*Amy runs off the closet side.*)

**Chilling:** (*He enters, carrying a plate of cookies.*) Here are the cookies you asked for, Stalwart. (*He hands the plate to Sidney. Then he begins to cough.*)

**Sidney:** Molasses and buttermilk might help that cough. You really ought to try it.

*(Offstage: a rapping on a door.)*

**Chilling:** Ah! That must be my guest. Don't go away, Stalwart. Just—ENJOY—your tea. (*He goes out.*)

**Sidney:** That must be the President of Wakowako! I've got to get him out of here as quickly as I can!

**Chilling:** (*He enters, followed by the President of Wakowako.*) Yes, indeed, Mr. President, you're right on time. Do come in. We can take care of our business right away.

**President:** But you have another guest! I do not wish to intrude.

**Chilling:** He's no guest! He's a—um—ah—a magazine reporter, name of Stalwart.

**President:** (*He bows to Sidney who bows back.*) Mr. Stalwart.

**Chilling:** Do sit down, Mr. President. (*He goes behind his table.*) Those papers are right here . . . (*He shuffles through the papers on the table.*) somewhere.

**President:** (*He sits down.*) Do not hurry yourself, Dr. Chilling. My journey has been a long one. I should welcome a few moments of rest.

**Sidney:** Er . . . would you like a cookie, Mr. President? They look very good. (*He offers the plate to the President.*)

**President:** Thank you. (*He takes a cookie.*) But really, I am thirsty. You will not mind if I drink this? (*He picks up the glass and begins to lift it to his mouth.*)

**Sidney:** Mr. President!

**President:** (*He lowers the glass and looks at Sidney.*) Yes?

**Sidney:** Ah—Mr. President, you don't want to drink that.

**President:** I beg your pardon?

**Sidney:** There's a fly in it.

**President:** A fly? (*He looks into the glass.*) I don't see any fly.

**Sidney:** No? Well, it's one of those very small ones. You know, the kind that bite when you're not looking. I wouldn't want you to get a bite on your tongue. I had one once, right here. . . . (*He sticks out his tongue at the President and points to a spot on it.*)

**Chilling:** (*He coughs.*) Mr. President! I think that before you drink anything we ought to sign the papers.

**President:** Perhaps you are right, Dr. Chilling. (*He puts the glass down on the table.*) After all, that is why I am here.

**Chilling:** (*He shuffles through the papers some more.*) I was *sure* those papers were here! (*He coughs again.*)

**Sidney:** Your cough is getting worse, Dr. Chilling. If I were you . . .

**Chilling:** (*He coughs several times.*) That's one thing I can be thankful for, Stalwart. You are NOT me! Excuse me, Mr. President. I must have taken the papers into the other room. I'll go get them. (*He goes out, coughing.*)

**Sidney:** Mr. President, I would advise you to leave here—right now!

**President:** Leave? Right now? Mr. Stalwart, you overstep yourself!

**Sidney:** Perhaps I should introduce myself.

**President:** But we've already met!

**Sidney:** Not really. You met my *disguise*. Actually, I'm Sidney Stalwart, Topnotch Secret Detective!

**President:** Secret Detective?

**Sidney:** Yes. From the Worldwide Secret Detective Agency. (*He bows.*)

(*Sidney goes to the closet side and pantomimes opening the door, and Amy enters.*)

**Sidney:** And this is Amy Truegood. She's a Secret Detective, too. Dr. Chilling had her locked in the closet.

**President:** (*He shakes his head in confusion.*) I don't understand any of this!

**Amy:** If you read the fine print on this contract that Dr. Chilling wants you to sign, you'll understand. (*She hands the papers to the President.*)

**President:** Let me see . . . (*He finds the place on the paper and reads aloud.*) "I hereby agree that the signing of this document shall make Dr. Amos Chilling the President of Wakowako and all the money in the treasury shall then belong to him." Why—why—this is terrible! Dr. Chilling must have stones in his head!

**Sidney:** Actually, stones in his bedrooms would be more accurate. Stones that once were PEOPLE.

**Amy:** Yes. That's what he was planning for me. And that's exactly what he is planning for you—as soon as you sign these papers.

**President:** (*He jumps up.*) Oh, no!

**Sidney:** Unfortunately, it's "oh, yes." Unless you leave right away, that is.

**President:** You are right, Mr. Stalwart. Good-bye, then, and thank you. (*He bows to Sidney who bows back.*)

**Amy:** I'll see you safely out, Mr. President.

(*They go out.*)

**Chilling:** (*He enters.*) That's strange, I can't seem to find . . . (*He looks around.*) Why, where's the President?

**Sidney:** Er . . . he couldn't wait. He had somewhere to go.

**Amy:** (*She enters.*) You have somewhere to go too, Dr. Chilling. To the POLICE!

**Chilling:** (*He whirls around and sees Amy.*) You! How did you get out of the closet? (*He starts to cough.*) I'll fix you! (*He coughs several times.*) I'll fix you both! Snoopy Secret Detectives! (*He coughs very hard and several times at once.*) My throat! (*He grabs the glass and begins to drink.*)

**Sidney:** Dr. Chilling, don't drink that! It's your . . .

(*Chilling drinks. As he does so, he slowly turns to "stone," becoming rigid. Both of his arms are bent at the elbows. From this moment on, he does not move.*)

**Amy:** It's too late, Sidney! He's become one of his own statues!

**Sidney:** So I see. Hmmm. (*He walks all around Chilling, looking at him.*) Amy, don't we owe the Boss a birthday present?

**Amy:** You mean . . . ?

**Sidney:** Yes. A Secret Detective should never leave a stone unturned. Help me carry him out, Amy.

(*They each lift Chilling by an elbow and carry him out.*)

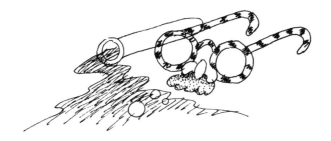

# THE CASE OF THE KIDNAPPED NEPHEW

## Characters

Court Clerk
Judge Alexander Fairman
Timothy Crane
Ms. Garfield, attorney for
the accused
Mr. Bradbury, prosecuting
attorney

Pamela Madison
Edith Allwell
Jonathan Slote
Brian Farley

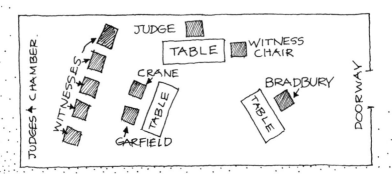

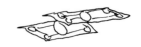

## Setting, properties, production notes

The scene is a courtroom. There are three tables and ten chairs. A gavel is on the judge's table. Pamela Madison walks with the aid of a cane (or stick) and carries a purse containing a letter in an envelope and a folded piece of yellow paper. Brian is wearing one green sock and one red sock. Each attorney has a folder of papers.

The Judge's chambers are to the audience's left, the doorway is to the audience's right. The Court Clerk and the Judge enter and exit from the Judge's chambers. All others enter and exit on the doorway side.

General note: The attorneys stand while they are questioning witnesses.

**As the play begins** _____

Everyone except the Court Clerk and the Judge enters. Garfield and Timothy are talking to each other. The witnesses are talking among themselves. They sit down—Garfield and Timothy are at the audience's left, and Bradbury is at the audience's right.

---

**Timothy:** This whole thing is crazy! I can't believe it's happening. I'm on trial for something I didn't do!

**Garfield:** You know you didn't do it, Tim, and I know it. But the only way we're going to be able to prove it is to discover who did!

**Clerk:** (*The clerk enters and stands, facing the audience, in front of the judge's table.*) Hear ye, hear ye, court is now in session. Judge Alexander Fairman presiding. All rise.

(*Everyone stands up. The judge comes in and sits down. Then everyone except the clerk sits down.*)

**Clerk:** The People versus Timothy Crane! (*The clerk sits down.*)

**Judge:** Timothy Crane, you are charged with kidnapping and extortion. How do you plead?

**Timothy:** (*He stands up.*) Not guilty, Your Honor. (*He sits down.*)

**Judge:** The clerk will enter the plea in the record. Ms. Garfield, as counsel for the defense, are you ready to proceed?

**Garfield:** (*She stands.*) Yes, Your Honor.

**Judge:** Mr. Bradbury, as prosecutor for the People, are you ready to proceed?

**Bradbury:** (*He stands up.*) Yes, Your Honor.

**Judge:** Very well. Begin then, please, Mr. Bradbury.

(*Ms. Garfield sits down.*)

**Bradbury:** (*He walks back and forth while he is talking.*) Your Honor, the People will prove that Timothy Crane did, on the 22nd of May this year, kidnap Brian Farley and extort money for his release from Mr. Farley's aunt, Mrs. Pamela Madison. To begin testimony, I call my first witness, Pamela Madison.

(*Pamela rises with difficulty and walks haltingly, leaning on her cane, to the witness chair and stands in front of it.*)

**Clerk:** (*The clerk stands.*) Do you swear to tell the truth, the whole truth, and nothing but the truth?

**Pamela:** I do. (*She sits down. So does the clerk.*)

**Bradbury:** Mrs. Madison, you are a writer, is that correct? And Timothy Crane is your secretary?

**Pamela:** Yes, that's correct. Tim is my secretary and research assistant. As you can see, I'm not able to get around easily—I have chronic arthritis. So Tim goes here and there on errands for me.

**Bradbury:** I see. Now, Mrs. Madison, will you please tell us in your own words what occurred on the 22nd of May.

**Pamela:** Well, Tim had gone out and I don't like to be alone in the house, so my friend Edith Allwell had come to stay with me. I was waiting for my nephew Brian to arrive from England. Earlier that day I'd received a telegram from him telling me not to meet him at the airport, that he would take a cab. Then, shortly before noon, the doorbell rang, and a messenger hand-delivered a letter. As soon as he put the envelope in my hand, he left—even before I had time to open it. The letter stated that Brian had been kidnapped!

**Bradbury:** Do you have that letter?

**Pamela:** Yes. (*She opens her purse and pulls out the envelope.*) Here it is.

**Bradbury:** Read it aloud, please.

**Pamela:** (*She takes the letter out of the envelope and reads.*) "If you want to see your nephew Brian alive, put ten thousand dollars in a suitcase and wait for further instructions. Do not call the police."

**Bradbury:** Your Honor, I would like to have the letter entered as the People's exhibit A.

**Judge:** It is so ordered.

**Bradbury:** (*He takes the letter from Pamela and hands it to the clerk.*) Go on, Mrs. Madison, what happened next?

**Pamela:** For a while, I didn't know what to do. I was terribly frightened. And I was afraid to call the police for fear that something would happen to Brian. Then I remembered that I *had* enough money. I own several racehorses and the day before I'd sold one to Admiral Denay. He'd paid me in cash. I got the money from my safe, and my friend Edith got one of my suitcases from the closet. I put the money inside and waited for further instructions. About an hour later the doorbell rang again. But this time there wasn't any messenger. There was just an envelope on the doorstep. It contained the instructions.

**Bradbury:** What were you instructed to do?

**Pamela:** To take the suitcase of money and put it in back of the newsstand at the corner. The letter said that if I did as I was told within ten minutes, Brian would be freed.

**Bradbury:** And did you follow the instructions?

**Pamela:** Yes, of course! Edith took the suitcase there for me since I'm unable to carry anything heavy while I'm walking.

**Bradbury:** And was Brian freed?

**Pamela:** Yes. He arrived at my home about an hour later.

**Bradbury:** Mrs. Madison, where was your secretary, Timothy Crane, at this time?

**Pamela:** I don't know. He had come to me quite early that morning and asked if he might have the day off. He seemed quite nervous about something. I told him he could, and he left immediately.

**Bradbury:** I see. Now, Mrs. Madison, who besides yourself knew that your nephew Brian was due to arrive that day?

**Pamela:** Only Tim and, of course, my friend Edith.

**Bradbury:** Tell me, Mrs. Madison, did Timothy Crane know what your nephew looked like?

**Pamela:** I would think so. When Brian wrote and said he was coming, he enclosed his picture so I'd recognize him. The picture had been on the mantel over the fireplace since I got it about two weeks before.

**Bradbury:** Thank you. (*He turns toward Garfield.*) Your witness. (*He sits down.*)

**Garfield:** (*She walks toward Pamela while she is talking.*) Mrs. Madison, could you describe the messenger who brought the ransom note?

**Pamela:** Not really. I couldn't see his face at all. He was bundled up in a rain slicker and hat—you know, the kind that covers most of your face. And I really wasn't paying much attention to him. (*She stops and thinks for a moment.*) I did notice that he had on one red sock and one green sock. I remember thinking how peculiar that was.

**Garfield:** So the messenger could have been anybody at all?

**Pamela:** Yes.

**Garfield:** You say that Timothy Crane was the only one besides your friend Ms. Allwell who knew that Brian was arriving from England. But a great many people—almost everyone—knew about the *money* you had, isn't that true?

**Pamela:** Yes, I suppose so. It had been in the papers that morning. Admiral Denay is a bit eccentric in that he always pays cash for the racehorses he buys, and newspaper reporters like that kind of story.

**Garfield:** Thank you, that's all. (*She goes back to her seat and sits down.*)

**Bradbury:** (*He rises.*) One question on redirect, Your Honor.

**Judge:** Proceed, Mr. Bradbury.

**Bradbury:** Mrs. Madison, could you say definitely that the messenger was *not* Timothy Crane? Think before you answer.

**Pamela:** (*She thinks for a second.*) No, I couldn't say that.

**Judge:** You may step down, Mrs. Madison.

(*Pamela gets up and goes back to her original seat.*)

**Bradbury:** My next witness is Ms. Edith Allwell.

(*Edith gets up and walks to the witness chair and stands in front of it.*)

**Clerk:** (*The clerk stands.*) Do you swear to tell the truth, the whole truth, and nothing but the truth?

**Edith:** I do. (*She sits down. So does the clerk.*)

**Bradbury:** Ms. Allwell, are you acquainted with Timothy Crane?

**Edith:** Yes, of course. He's been Mrs. Madison's secretary for a number of years. And I am a regular visitor at her home.

**Bradbury:** Did you ever have occasion to see him elsewhere?

**Edith:** Yes, as a matter of fact. Like Mrs. Madison, I own some racehorses. I go to the racetrack quite often. And I've seen Tim there—bumped into him, you might say.

**Bradbury:** And did he win or lose?

**Garfield:** (*She rises.*) Objection! That's immaterial, Your Honor!

**Bradbury:** (*He turns toward the judge.*) Your Honor, I intend to show that it is not. In fact, it may be the *reason* for this crime.

**Judge:** Very well. Objection overruled. You may answer the question, Ms. Allwell.

**Edith:** I've no idea whether Tim won or lost.

**Bradbury:** Hmmm. All right. Now let's go back to the day of the kidnapping. What time had you arrived at Mrs. Madison's home?

**Edith:** Oh, I'd say around 10 A.M., or so. She'd called me shortly after nine, and I got there as quickly as I could. I stayed with her until sometime after Brian arrived—about an hour or so.

**Bradbury:** Were you there when Timothy Crane returned from wherever he'd been?

**Edith:** Yes, I was.

**Bradbury:** And when was that?

**Edith:** About half an hour after Brian came in. We were listening to Brian tell about what had happened to him when Tim came in.

**Bradbury:** And how did he seem to you?

**Edith:** He seemed to be agitated, nervous. But we were so taken up with Brian that I didn't pay too much attention to Tim.

**Bradbury:** Thank you. Your witness, Ms. Garfield. (*He goes to his seat.*)

**Garfield:** Ms. Allwell, you say Timothy Crane seemed agitated. Yet, you admit you weren't paying too much attention to his mood.

**Edith:** That's true.

**Garfield:** Weren't *you* agitated at that point, given the events of the day?

**Edith:** Indeed I was! My heart was still jumping. I can't remember ever being so frightened or upset!

**Garfield:** Why, then, wouldn't Timothy Crane be agitated? After all, he had been in Mrs. Madison's employ for a long time. Certainly, you would credit him with caring about her.

**Bradbury:** (*He rises.*) Objection! That's calling for an opinion!

**Judge:** Objection sustained. The witness will not answer the question.

**Garfield:** No further questions. (*She returns to her seat.*)

**Judge:** You may step down, Ms. Allwell. Mr. Bradbury, call your next witness.

(*Edith goes back to her seat.*)

**Bradbury:** (*He rises.*) I call Jonathan Slote.

(*Jonathan gets up and walks to the witness chair.*)

**Clerk:** (*The clerk stands.*) Do you swear to tell the truth, the whole truth, and nothing but the truth?

**Jonathan:** I do. (*He sits down. So does the clerk.*)

**Bradbury:** Mr. Slote, what is your occupation?

**Jonathan:** I'm—I work for a literary agency. Mrs. Madison's agent is my employer.

**Bradbury:** And do you know Mrs. Madison's secretary, Timothy Crane?

**Jonathan:** Oh, yes. We come from the same town in Illinois. I've known him all my life. In fact, it was he who recommended me to my employer.

**Bradbury:** And do you have occasion to see him often?

**Jonathan:** Yes, sir. We have the same day off and generally spend it together.

**Bradbury:** And what do you and Mr. Crane do on your days off?

**Jonathan:** Usually, we go to the races. We both like to bet on the horses.

**Bradbury:** Mr. Slote, do you know if Mr. Crane won or lost at the races?

**Jonathan:** Well, lately he'd been losing.

**Bradbury:** I see. Mr. Slote, do you know how much money he had lost?

**Jonathan:** Not exactly. It has to be quite a lot, though. Because he's borrowed money from me—he owes me over a thousand dollars.

**Bradbury:** And has he expressed an intention to repay you?

**Jonathan:** Oh, yes. He told me that he'd have it for me very soon.

**Bradbury:** When did he tell you that?

**Jonathan:** Two days before Brian Farley was kidnapped.

**Bradbury:** Thank you. Your witness. (*He returns to his seat.*)

**Garfield:** (*She rises.*) I have only one question for Mr. Slote. Tell me, Mr. Slote, since you have known the defendant so long, do you think him capable of committing this crime?

**Bradbury:** (*He rises.*) Objection, Your Honor! Opinion!

**Judge:** Hmmm. I think I'll overrule your objection, Mr. Bradbury. The witness may answer.

**Garfield:** Mr. Slote?

**Jonathan:** No, I don't *think* so.

**Garfield:** Thank you. No further questions. (*She sits down.*)

**Judge:** You may step down, Mr. Slote. Before you call your next witness, Mr. Bradbury, we will take a recess.

**Clerk:** (*The clerk stands up.*) All rise!

(*Everyone stands as the judge goes out the chambers side, followed by the clerk. Then everyone but Garfield and Timothy go out the doorway side. Garfield and Timothy sit down.*)

**Timothy:** It doesn't look good for me, does it?

**Garfield:** No, Tim, I'm afraid it doesn't. (*She thinks for a second.*) The nephew will probably be the next witness. What's he like?

**Timothy:** He seems nice enough. A bit down on his luck at the moment, I'd guess from his conversation. But he's got a good sense of humor. Takes after his father, according to Mrs. Madison. She says he has all the family traits.

**Garfield:** What do you mean, all?

**Timothy:** Oh, just the odd things that occur in some families. You know, allergies and that sort of thing. Mrs. Madison says that all the men in her family are color-blind, hate squash, and are allergic to strawberries.

**Garfield:** Hmmmm. Color-blind. (*She thinks for a moment.*) I wonder . . .

(*Everyone except the judge and the clerk returns to the courtroom. They don't all come at once—they straggle in. When everyone is in his or her seat the clerk comes in and faces them all.*)

**Clerk:** All rise!

(*Everyone stands up. The judge comes in and takes his seat.*)

**Clerk:** Be seated.

(*Everyone, including the clerk, sits down.*)

**Judge:** Mr. Bradbury, call your witness.

**Bradbury:** (*He rises.*) Mr. Brian Farley.

(*Brian comes to the witness chair and stands in front of it.*)

**Clerk:** (*The clerk stands.*) Do you swear to tell the truth, the whole truth, and nothing but the truth?

**Brian:** I do. (*He sits down. So does the clerk.*)

**Bradbury:** Mr. Farley, please tell the court what happened to you on May 22nd.

**Brian:** Yes, sir. Just before my plane landed, the airflight attendant told me that I'd got a message not to go to my aunt's house. I was to meet her at a different address. I took a cab there. No sooner had I rung the bell, when the door opened and somebody grabbed me. I never did see the man's face. Before I knew what was happening, I was bound, gagged, and blindfolded. Then I heard the man go out. He came back some time later, pushed me out the door, and into a car. We drove for quite some time. Then he stopped the car, untied my hands, and pushed me out. He drove away before I could get the blindfold off. When I finally managed to remove it, I found that I was back at the airport. I hailed a cab and went to my aunt's house.

**Bradbury:** Thank you, Mr. Farley. Your witness, Ms. Garfield. (*He sits down.*)

**Garfield:** (*She is talking to herself in a loud whisper.*) Something isn't . . . but what is it? (*She rises.*) I would like to reserve my cross examination until later, Your Honor. (*She sits down.*)

**Judge:** Very well. Call another witness, Mr. Bradbury.

(*Brian returns to his seat.*)

**Bradbury:** (*He rises.*) The prosecution has no other witnesses, Your Honor. (*He sits down.*)

**Judge:** Then we will hear from the defense. Ms. Garfield.

**Garfield:** (*She rises.*) The defense calls Timothy Crane.

(*Timothy goes to the witness chair and stands in front of it.*)

**Clerk:** (*The clerk stands.*) Do you swear to tell the truth, the whole truth, and nothing but the truth?

**Timothy:** I do. (*He sits down. So does the clerk.*)

**Garfield:** Mr. Crane, please tell the court what you did on the day in question.

**Timothy:** I left the house a little after nine in the morning and went to the racetrack. I was to meet a guy I know. He'd promised to give me a good solid tip on the sixth race. And I needed that tip. I'd lost a lot of money, including most of what I'd borrowed from my friend, Jon Slote. I figured that with a good tip, I could make back what I'd lost—and maybe more. But the guy never showed up. I hunted all over for him. Then the races started. I bet—and lost. I felt sick so I went home, back to Mrs. Madison's.

**Garfield:** Did you see anyone you knew at the racetrack?

**Timothy:** No. If it had been my regular day off, I probably would have—the same people seem to be there all the time. But this was a different day. Besides, I was busy looking for the guy I was supposed to meet. I didn't pay any attention to who was there.

**Garfield:** Were you aware that it was the day that Mrs. Madison's nephew was to arrive?

**Timothy:** Yes. His telegram had come just before I left the house.

**Garfield:** (*She walks back and forth for a moment, thinking. Then she stops.*) Mr. Crane, did you read the telegram?

**Timothy:** Yes. I open all the mail. As soon as I read it, I gave it to Mrs. Madison.

**Garfield:** Do you happen to know what she did with it?

**Timothy:** Hmmm. I think she put it in her purse.

**Garfield:** (*She turns toward the judge.*) Your Honor, if Mrs. Madison still has the telegram in her purse, perhaps we might see it?

**Judge:** (*He nods, then turns and looks at Pamela.*) Mrs. Madison, do you have that telegram?

**Pamela:** I'll see, Your Honor. (*She opens her purse and searches through it. After a second or two she pulls out a folded piece of yellow paper.*) Yes. Here it is.

**Judge:** Give it to the clerk, please.

(*The clerk takes the telegram and brings it to Ms. Garfield.*)

**Garfield:** Thank you. (*She takes it from the clerk and reads aloud.*) It says: "Arriving 1:30 P.M. Do not meet me. Will take a cab." And it's signed Brian. (*She hands it to Timothy.*) Is this the telegram you saw?

(*He looks at it.*) Yes, it is. (*He hands it back to Garfield.*)

**Garfield:** Thank you, Mr. Crane. I have no further questions. Your witness, Mr. Bradbury. (*She returns to her seat and puts the telegram on the table in front of her.*)

**Bradbury:** Your testimony was very interesting, Mr. Crane. But do you really expect us to believe that you saw no one you knew at the racetrack? After all, it is a place you go often.

**Timothy:** Yes, but I didn't see anyone I knew that day.

**Bradbury:** Of course, you didn't. Because you weren't there! You never went to the racetrack. Instead, you were holding Brian Farley prisoner! You knew your employer had a great deal of cash on hand and that she would gladly exchange it for the safe return of her nephew.

**Timothy:** No! That's not true! I didn't do it! I didn't!

**Bradbury:** I submit that you did, Mr. Crane. No further questions. (*He returns to his seat.*)

**Judge:** You may step down, Mr. Crane. Ms. Garfield, call your next witness.

*(Crane returns to his seat.)*

**Garfield:** *(She rises.)* I have no other witnesses, Your Honor. But at this time I'd like to have Brian Farley recalled to the stand for cross-examination.

**Judge:** Very well. Brian Farley, take the stand.

*(Brian goes to the witness chair and sits down.)*

**Judge:** Remember, Mr. Farley, you are still under oath.

**Brian:** Yes, Your Honor.

**Garfield:** Mr. Farley, before you left England, you sent a telegram to your aunt not to meet your plane. Why was that?

**Brian:** I wanted to save her a trip to the airport.

**Garfield:** That was very considerate of you. By the way, what time did your plane arrive?

**Brian:** One-thirty in the afternoon.

**Garfield:** And it was a direct, non-stop flight from England?

**Brian:** Yes.

**Garfield:** (*She walks over to the table and picks up the telegram.*) Can you tell me then, Mr. Farley, how your aunt received this *telegram* from you and not a cablegram? Telegrams are *land* wires, not overseas wires.

**Brian:** Why—uhhh . . .

**Garfield:** Mr. Farley, how long have you been out of work?

**Brian:** About six months. But I don't see what that has to do with anything.

**Garfield:** Let's let the court decide that. Tell me, if you've not worked in six months, where did you get the money for the trip?

**Brian:** I—I—borrowed it. I'm to pay it back within a month.

**Garfield:** I see. Mr. Farley, what would you say if I contended that you were never kidnapped at all? That you, in fact, landed in the United States in the morning, saw the newspaper report of your aunt's sale of a racehorse to Admiral Denay, guessed that she had a lot of cash on hand—and cooked up this scheme to rob her?

**Brian:** That's ridiculous!

**Garfield:** Is it? Tell me, Mr. Farley, what color socks are you wearing?

**Brian:** What . . . ? (*He pulls up both legs of his pants so that his socks show and looks down at them.*) They're green. But I don't see . . .

**Garfield:** No, *you* don't. But perhaps the court will. You are not wearing two green socks, Mr. Farley. Only one is green. The other is red. You can't tell the difference because you are color-blind.

**Brian:** So what?

**Garfield:** Isn't it strange that the messenger who brought the ransom note also wore one red sock and one green one? Perhaps he, too, is color-blind. Or perhaps, Mr. Farley, *you* were the messenger!

**Brian:** I—I—oh, what's the use! Yes, I did it. Just the way you said. I thought no one would find out! (*He covers his face with his hands.*) I'll give the money back!

**Judge:** (*He pounds the gavel.*) Mr. Bradbury, I think a motion to dismiss the case against Mr. Crane is in order.

**Bradbury:** (*He rises.*) I so move, Your Honor.

**Judge:** Motion granted. Case dismissed! (*He pounds the gavel once.*) The clerk will escort Mr. Farley to the bailiff where he will be advised of his rights and then removed to the jail.

(*The clerk goes over to the witness stand and takes Brian's arm and escorts him out the doorway side.*)

**Judge:** Court is adjourned. (*He gets up and goes out.*)

(*Everyone, except Timothy and Garfield, rises and heads for the doorway, talking among themselves.*)

**Timothy:** (*He turns to Garfield.*) I don't know how to thank you . . .

(*On her way to the door, Pamela has stopped next to Timothy's chair. She puts her hand on his shoulder and faces Garfield.*)

**Pamela:** Let me add my thanks, too. Though it hurts to know that my own nephew tried to rob me, it makes me feel better to know that my trust in Tim all these years hasn't been misplaced.

**Garfield:** No thanks are necessary. Tim's telling me that Brian is color-blind was what gave me the answer. The path to truth, in this case, was marked in red and green.

(*Garfield and Timothy rise. Timothy takes Pamela's arm and all three go out together.*)

# Puzzling Stories to Read

Avi. *No More Magic*. New York: Pantheon, 1975. Was it a real warlock who was seen riding Chris' missing bike on Halloween night? And was it the warlock who was responsible for Muffin's parents being gone?

Brookins, Dana. *Alone in Wolf Hollow*. New York: Houghton Mifflin/Clarion Books, 1978. Orphaned Bart and Arnie Cadle thought being abandoned by their uncle was real trouble—until they found themselves face-to-face with a murderer.

Corbett, Scott. *Take a Number*. New York: E. P. Dutton, 1974. When Adrienne is kidnapped by her gambler-stepfather, Dee's only hope of locating her is dependent on "telepathy."

Fleischman, Sid. *The Ghost on Saturday Night*. Boston: Atlantic-Little, Brown, 1974. Opie's ability to find his way in a tule fog helps him to solve this funny mystery involving a "ghost raising."

Hildick, E. W. *The Case of the Secret Scribbler*. New York: Macmillan, 1978. Jack McGurk and his Detective Organization believe they have found scribbled evidence of a robbery in the planning. But who is going to be robbed? And can McGurk's Organization prevent it? One of a series.

McHargue, Georgess. *The Talking Table Mystery*. New York: Doubleday, 1977. A table that rapped, a silver piccolo, and some pages from an old diary spelled trouble for Annie Conway and her best friend, Howard Kappelman.

Meyers, Susan. *The Mysterious Bender Bones.* New York: Doubleday, 1970. Kermit Fox wanted to know two things: Why had Mrs. Bender hired him to dig up her cellar? And who was the mysterious stranger skulking around the island?

Nixon, Joan Lowery. *The Mysterious Red Tape Gang.* New York: G. P. Putnam's Sons, 1974. Mike, Linda Jean, and the rest of their gang inadvertently stumble into danger in their secret efforts to help their community get rid of some nuisances.

Roberts, Willo Davis. *The View from the Cherry Tree.* New York: Atheneum, 1975. If Rob Mallory had really seen his next-door neighbor being murdered, had the murderer also seen him?

Sharmat, Marjorie Weinman. *Nate the Great Goes Undercover.* New York: Coward, McCann & Geoghegan, 1974. In this funny, easily read mystery, Nate the Great tries to discover who is making nightly raids on the garbage cans. One of a series.

Sobol, Donald. *Encyclopedia Brown Saves the Day.* New York: Elsevier/Nelson, 1970. Are you as good as Encyclopedia Brown at spotting clues? The solutions to each of the ten short mysteries are in the back of the book. One of a series.

Yolen, Jane, compiler. *Shape Shifters.* New York: Houghton Mifflin/Clarion Books, 1978. People who take on animal forms are the subjects of these sometimes funny, sometimes scary short stories.

## About the Author

SUE ALEXANDER was born in Tucson, Arizona, and grew up in Chicago where she attended Drake University and Northwestern University. Ms. Alexander began writing at age eight and in recent years has published ten books for young people, including *Small Plays for Special Days* and *Small Plays for You and a Friend* for Clarion. The mother of three children, she now lives in Canoga Park, California, and is Board Chairperson of The Society of Children's Book Writers.

## About the Artist

TOM HUFFMAN grew up in Lexington, Kentucky, and now lives in New York City. Interested in art since he was a small child, Mr. Huffman received his B.A. in Fine Arts from the University of Kentucky and attended the School of Visual Arts in New York City. A full time freelance artist, he has illustrated over fifteen books for children, among them Sue Alexander's *Small Plays for You and a Friend*.

ABCDEFGHIJ—VB—876543210/80